Get Connected:
Make a Friendship Bracelet

By Dana Meachen Rau

NORWOOD HOUSE PRESS

Norwood House Press
PO Box 316598
Chicago, Illinois 60631

For information regarding Norwood House Press, please visit our Web site at:

www.norwoodhousepress.com or call 866-565-2900.

Acknowledgement
The author would like to thank Peter Jemison, historic site manager, Ganondagan

Picture Credits:
Benjwong/Pubic Domain, 13; Danny de Bruyne, 8; Dorieo/Public Domain, 6; Rowshan Dowlatabadi, 20; Tamia Dowlatabadi, 17 (bottom), 36 (inset), 37; Lloyd Gerald, 24 (right), 25, 26, 29 (right), 31, 32, 33, 34, 35 (left), 36, 38 (right), 40–42, 43 (left); cc-by-sa3.0*/Faith Goble/Wikimedia, 16 (right); Craig Hauger 38 (left); Roger Kirby, 14; Library of Congress, 10, 15; Melodi T, 18; Polaris999/Public Domain, 17 (top); Public domain, 5, 7, 9, 11; Dana Meachen Rau, cover, 19, 20 (inset), 22, 24 (left), 27–28, 29 (left), 30 (left), 35 (right), 39, 43 (right); Irum Shahid, 16 (left); cc-by-sa2.0/Satbir Singh/Wikimedia, 12; Snickup, 30 (right); Sumos, 4
*cc-by-sa= Creative Commons by Share Alike License

LIBRARY OF CONGRESS CATALOGING-IN-PUBLICATION DATA

Rau, Dana Meachen, 1971-
  Get connected : make a friendship bracelet / Dana Meachen Rau.
    p. cm. -- (Adventure guides)
  Includes bibliographical references and index.
  Summary: "Reviews the meaning and history of jewelry over time as well as step-by-step instructions for creating beaded bracelets, also known as friendship bracelets. Instructions include how to look for materials, threading the beads, and creating a loom. Glossary, additional resources and index"--Provided by publisher.
  ISBN-13: 978-1-59953-385-8 (library edition : alk. paper)
  ISBN-10: 1-59953-385-5 (library edition : alk. paper)
  1. Beadwork. 2. Bracelets. I. Title.
  TT860.R37 2010
  745.594'2--dc22
                                                                2010010404

Manufactured in the United States of America in North Mankato, Minnesota.
158N—072010

Table of Contents

Jewelry is a time-honored gift among loved ones and friends.

Chapter 1

Stone, Gold, and Shell:
Jewelry That Sends a Message

Giving a gift is a way people show they care for each other. Jewelry is one of the most popular gifts for holidays, birthdays, or other special occasions. Since early in history, people have been giving gifts of jewelry.

The Value and Meaning of Jewelry

One of the most famous gifts of jewelry is a necklace that is now part of the Smithsonian Institution's gem collection. The Smithsonian Institution is a group of museums in Washington, D.C. In 1811 the French emperor Napoléon gave his second wife a necklace to celebrate the birth of their son. This necklace made of diamonds is worth millions of dollars.

Marie Louis of Austria, empress of France was Napoléon's second wife.

Jewelry like this was used to mark important occasions because it was considered valuable. The rarer the material jewelry is made from, the more value it holds. Historically, the materials of jewelry have varied depending on where cultures developed. Early cultures used bones, stones, or feathers. Craftspeople melted and molded gold and silver metal to make jewelry. Cultures near the shore might use shells or pearls. The Chinese were famous for their use of the stone jade. The artists of Venice, Italy, made beads of glass.

Diamonds are among the most valuable **gemstones**. One of the most famous diamonds in history is the Koh-i-noor diamond. It passed through the hands of many emperors and conquerors until the mid-1800s, when it became a part of the jewelry owned by the queen of England.

Because jewelry is valuable, it has been used throughout history for trade. A dowry is money and gifts that a new bride brings to her husband when they get married. Jewelry was often among the gifts. Europeans who arrived in Africa in the 15th century traded their glass beads to get supplies they needed. These trade beads were used as **currency** by the Europeans to buy gold, palm oil, and even slaves from Africa.

Besides being given or traded for its value, jewelry can also say something to others. In many cultures, the more jewelry a person wears, the more impor-

Throughout history, jewelry has been part of dowries for women like this young bride here.

tant they are. Kings, queens, and other leaders throughout history have been weighted down with crowns, rings, necklaces, collars, and other jewelry to declare their high status to others. Some jewelry communicates a warning. The wearers think it protects them from bad luck or illness. Jewelry can also show that someone is a part of a certain group or holds certain beliefs. For example, a cross communicates that someone is Christian.

Wearing certain jewelry carries meaning, such as wearing a cross.

Speaking with Wampum

Wampum beads were considered valuable by the Native Americans of the eastern woodlands. Archaeologists have found wampum that is thousands of years old. The Algonquin people along the Atlantic coast of the United States made white wampum beads from the center of a **whelk** shell. They made purple beads from the dark part of a **quahog** clam shell. They used these small white and purple beads to decorate their clothing. They wove wampum into jewelry such as bracelets, necklaces, and belts.

The Native Americans of New England and New York began to use

Wampum Keepers

If the **council** of Haudenosaunee leaders passed a law, it was recorded in a string or belt of wampum. The Keeper of the Wampum was in charge of remembering and reciting the laws recorded in wampum at council meetings. The order or arrangement of the beads helped the Keeper remember the laws.

Native American chiefs hold elaborate wampum belts.

wampum in other ways. They used it to communicate. The Haudenosaunee (ho-dee-no-SAW-nee) (Iroquois) used wampum to share messages. The designs on wampum belts held special meaning. White beads often **symbolized** health, peace, and friendship. Pur-

ple beads, however, were for more serious matters. They might even communicate **hostile** feelings. A certain arrangement of wampum on a belt invited others to come to a meeting. A belt with a white background and purple designs might have meant friendship or an **alliance**. But a belt with a purple background, or one painted red, might have declared war.

Native Americans also used wampum in meetings of the tribal nation's leaders. At these councils, wampum helped people record and remember important events or laws. It showed the order that the council members should be seated. Wampum also communicated a council member's leadership position. When he or she no longer held their position, the wampum was given to the next person to take that role. Recording something in wampum showed it was important enough to be remembered.

In the 1600s, Dutch, French, and British settlers came to North America from Europe to explore, trade, and start new lives. They came in contact with the Native American nations already living there. They soon realized how important wampum was to these nations.

So the settlers found another use for wampum. They needed a form of money. The metal coins they had used in Europe were not as readily available in America. They started using

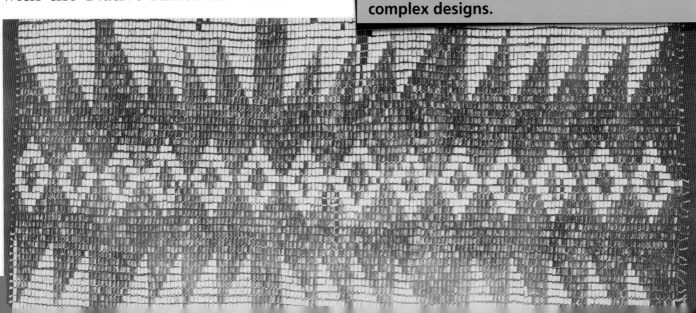

A close-up of a wampum belt reveals its complex designs.

wampum instead. They traded wampum with the Native Americans for items such as furs. They used it among each other to pay for goods and services. The use of wampum grew as trade routes and settlements moved farther west and south.

The Dutch started workshops that produced large amounts of wampum. A wampum factory opened in the early 1800s in New Jersey. **Counterfeit** wampum beads, made of glass instead of shell, were also produced.

When the Native Americans and the settlers made alliances with each other, they presented wampum belts to remember these important agreements. Wampum became valuable and meaningful to both the Native Americans and the settlers of North America.

Native Americans used beads in decorative arts. This decorative panel from a Nez Percé tribe's saddle is finely decorated with beads.

Honoring Friendship

George Washington presented a wampum belt to the Haudenosaunee (Iroquois) Confederacy in 1794. The house and the two figures in the center of the belt represented the Haudenosaunee. The other figures symbolized the first thirteen states of the United States of America. The belt marked a treaty between the U.S. government and the Native Americans to live in peace.

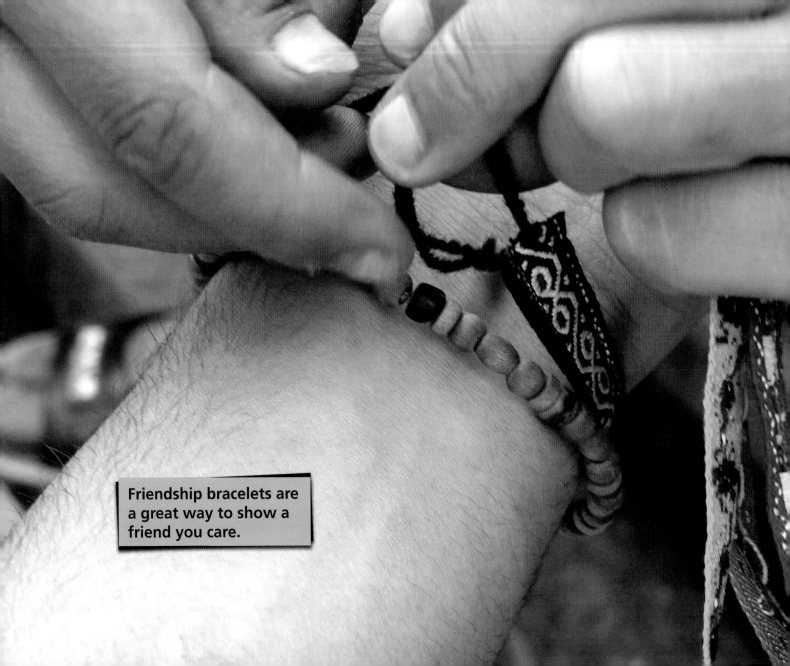

Friendship bracelets are a great way to show a friend you care.

Chapter 2

Getting Started:
Making a Bracelet for a Friend

In some myths and stories, gemstones hold special meaning. For example, some stories say that dark red garnets can protect you on a journey, that deep green emeralds keep you healthy, or that blue-green aquamarines can keep you safe at sea. Tibetan dzi (pronounced ZEE) beads are made from the stone called agate. Dzi beads have a more than 5000-year history in Tibet. These beads are thought to be powerful and protect the wearer. Some are decorated with white circles, called "eyes." The meaning of a bead depends on how many eyes it has. For example, a two-eyed bead means harmony.

We also use jewelry to communicate today. When two people get married,

This Tibetan dzi bead shows the white circle "eyes." Different numbers of eyes are said to carry different meanings.

Many people exchange wedding bands when they get married.

elry are also passed down through family members. Wearing a necklace from a grandparent, for example, is a special way of remembering him or her.

Sometimes friends give each other gifts. And some of the best presents are the kind you make yourself. Making a friendship bracelet is a great handmade gift.

they buy each other wedding rings. These rings are a symbol of their love and the promise they are making to each other. We give jewelry as gifts for birthdays or holidays to show others we care about them. Special pieces of jew-

Choosing Your Beads

Native Americans had to be careful when making shells into wampum beads, because shells can break easily. They cut the shell into small pieces. They drilled into one end, then the other, to form a hole through the middle. Then they smoothed the beads by rubbing them on a stone.

Today, we have many types of beads to choose from. Bead stores are fully stocked with beads and jewelry supplies. Craft stores often have aisles devoted to beading. You will find beads in bags, tubes, or on strands of thread. They come in all shapes and sizes and are made of many different materials.

You might like to use metal beads made of gold, silver, or less expensive metals. Glass beads are also very popular. The smallest round glass beads are called seed beads. Longer, tube-shaped glass beads are called bugle beads.

Clay is another bead material. Clay beads are often painted with designs.

A Zuni silversmith drills holes in beads.

Types of Bracelets

There are many types of bracelets. You can buy chain bracelets made of gold or silver. These close with a clasp. Charm bracelets are chain bracelets with larger links made to hold dangling charms. You can buy special charms to show off something about you, remember a place you visited, or honor an event in your life. A cuff is a very wide bracelet. A bangle is a solid ring and can be made of metal, plastic, or even wood. You might get a wristband bracelet at a sporting event or to support a cause. These are made of rubber and come in all different colors.

Bangles come in many patterns

Clay fimo beads come in many colors.

Polymer clay is a material you can use to make your own beads. You mold it in the shape and design you wish, then bake it until it is hard.

Wooden beads and plastic beads are also good for bracelet projects. They come in lots of shapes and sizes, too. You can find round ones, barrel-shaped

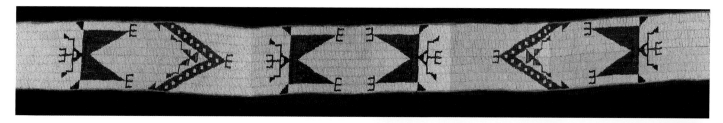

ones, shell shapes, animal shapes—almost any shape you can imagine.

The Story on String

Native American wampum beads were woven into belts and bracelets with thread. The long threads that run the length of the belt or bracelet are called warp threads. The Native Americans might have used milkweed, bark, or another type of plant fiber twisted together for warp threads. Sometimes they used **buckskin,** although that was not as strong. The warp threads are the main threads that hold the belt together.

The thread used to hold the beads onto the warp threads are called weft threads. For this, the Native Americans

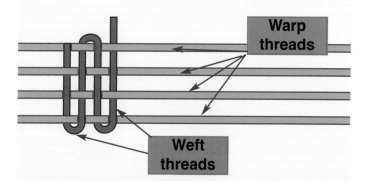

Friendship bracelets can use many different materials for stringing, including thread made from cotton or hemp.

used sinew. Sinew is a strong **cord** that connects an animal's muscles to its bones.

You can buy many types of thread and cord. Leather is a natural material and good for beading. There are also cords made of plastic or cotton. Embroidery floss is a type of thread that comes in hundreds of colors. You can also use thinner thread made for sewing. Clear, plastic thread seems to be "invisible." Or there is elastic thread which can stretch, making it easy to put a bracelet on or take it off. Hemp is a natural plant fiber used to make cord, too. You can buy it in its natural brown color or dyed in other colors.

To make a bracelet, you will need thread for the warp threads and for the weft threads. What kinds of threads to

Just the Thread

Some bracelets are made only of thread. Sailor-knot bracelets are made from rope. Sailors thought wearing them brought them good luck. **Macramé** is a knotting craft practiced for centuries. Weavers in the Middle East used to tie the extra threads around the edges of their woven pieces with knots to create a nicer border.

Some people make friendship bracelets by using knotting techniques. You just need embroidery floss and a simple knot to make bracelets striped with colors.

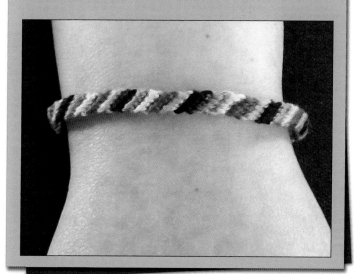

The colors and items chosen for a friendship bracelet can be inspired by many different things. A sunset, your friend's love of unusual stones or shells, or his or her favorite color can make a unique gift.

choose depends on the size of the beads you use. Warp threads can be thicker. But the weft thread has to be able to fit through the holes in your beads.

A Source of Inspiration

Before you start making a bracelet, think about the person you are making it for. What does your friend like? What do you want your bracelet to "say" to him or her?

Perhaps you can think of an event in your friendship that you want to remember. Maybe you were both on a soccer team together. Perhaps you were both in the school play. These events can help you decide the design of your bracelet.

You can make a bracelet in your friend's favorite colors. Or you can make stripes of your school colors. Maybe your friend likes to watch the sunset. You could make a bracelet with red, orange, and yellow. Even a simple friendship bracelet can have lots of meaning.

Chapter 3

Weaving with Thread and Beads

A wampum-style bracelet is a good project to learn weaving and beading techniques. The weaving technique is called single-thread weave. Start with a one-row bracelet made with large beads. Then try a bracelet with more rows and smaller beads so you can be more creative with your design.

These are the materials you will need to make a one-row bracelet:

✓ **Wooden beads or plastic pony beads** Pony beads look like large seed beads. They are round with a nice wide hole in the center. Any similar size beads with large openings will work for this project. A bag of pony beads costs about $5.00 or less.

✓ **Beading needle** A sewing needle will work, too. But it needs to be thin enough to fit easily through your beads. Beading needles cost about $1.50 for a set.

✓ **Hemp cord** Hemp comes in a variety of colors and styles. For this project, you will use it for both the warp and weft threads. Hemp comes in spools or packets for about $5.00 or less.

✓ **Measuring tape** You will be using this to measure your wrist size. You can buy a measuring tape in a sewing store or pharmacy for about $3.00. Or you can just put a piece of string around your wrist, mark it where the ends would meet, and then measure that length against a flat ruler.

✓ **Masking tape** Masking tape costs about $2.00 a roll.

✓ **Cardboard** You can get this for free from an old box or the back of an empty notebook.

✓ **Scissors**

Make a One-Row Bracelet

Step #1: Cutting the Cords

1. First, measure your wrist with the measuring tape.

2. For the warp threads, cut two lengths of hemp, each 12 inches (30.5cm) longer than your wrist measurement. For example, if your wrist is 6 inches (15.25cm) around, cut two 18-inch (45.75cm) lengths of hemp. This should be enough cord for the beaded part of the bracelet and the extra you will need for tying it off when you are done.

3. Next, cut another length of hemp twice the length of your warp threads. This will be your weft thread. For example, if your warp threads are 18 inches (45.75cm) long, your weft thread will need to be 36 inches (91.5cm) long.

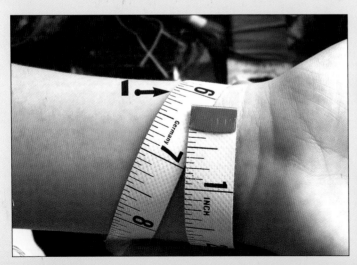

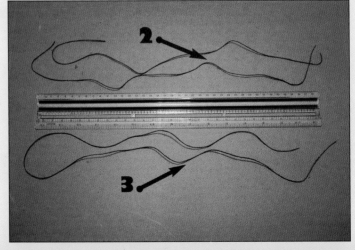

Step #2: Setting Up the Strings

To make wampum bracelets and belts, the Native Americans sometimes used a loom. A loom holds your project steady and anchors the warp threads. The loom also keeps the warp threads lined up and separated. With a loom, you are able to handle your work from above, below, and from the sides.

The bow loom used by the Native Americans looked like the bow people use for shooting arrows. It was made of a curved stick, with the warp threads tied onto each end. Here is how to make a simple bow loom of your own:

1. Cut a piece of cardboard about 3 inches (7.6cm) wide by 11 inches (28cm) long. Cut two slits in each end about ½ inch (1.3cm) apart.

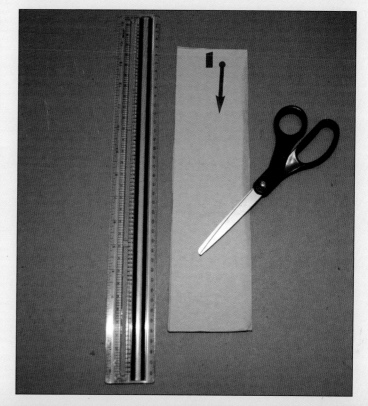

2. Slide the warp threads into the slots on one edge of the cardboard. Leave about 6 inches (15.2cm) of the thread ends hanging. Slide the other ends of the warp threads into the slots on the opposite edge of the cardboard. Pull them gently until about 6 inches (15.2cm) of those ends are hanging, too. Your cardboard will curve and form a bow shape.

3. If you wish, you can tape down the threads on the back of the loom with masking tape to hold them in place.

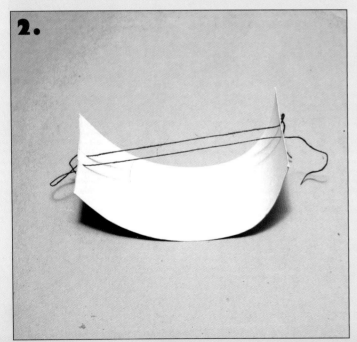

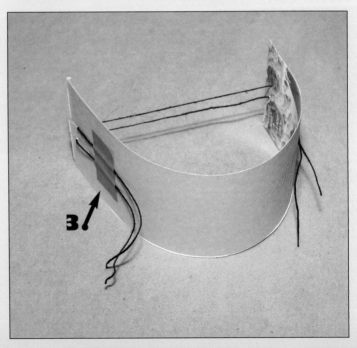

Step #3: The Basic Bracelet

1. To start, tie the end of the weft thread to Warp Thread One (the thread on the left) with a simple overhand knot. To tie an overhand knot, place the weft under Warp Thread One. Cross the end of the weft to form a loop. Tuck the end through the loop. Pull tight. Leave about a 6-inch (15.2cm) tail.

Tuck the tail through the slot for Warp Thread One. Push the knot to the top of Warp Thread One.

2. Pass the long end of the weft thread under both Warp Thread One and Warp Thread Two and toward the right. String a bead on the weft thread. Hold it in place between the two warp threads with one hand. Pull the weft thread tight.

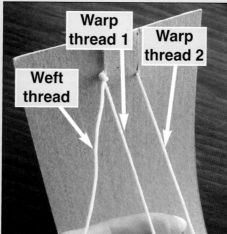
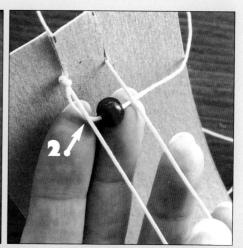

Weft thread

Warp thread 1

Warp thread 2

3. Now pass the weft thread back toward the left over Warp Thread Two, back through the bead, then over Warp Thread One. Pull the thread tight. Now your weft thread has returned to the left side, and your bead is securely in place between the warp threads.

4. To add a second bead, pass the weft thread under both warp threads toward the right. String on a bead and hold it in place between the warp threads.

5. Pass the weft thread over the warp threads and back through the bead toward the left. Pull to tighten.

Repeat steps 4 and 5 until the beaded part measures the same as your wrist measurement.

Be sure that as you add each bead, you keep the string tight and pulled all the way through the bead. If the weft thread gets frayed, you can snip off the frayed end or wrap the end with a small ring of masking tape so it is stiff, like a shoelace. This will help you poke it through the beads.

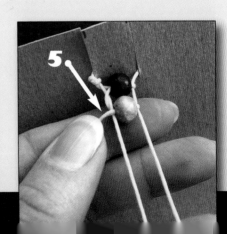

Step #4: Finishing Up

1. When the beaded part of the bracelet reaches the right length, slip the warp threads off the ends of the loom. On the top end, gather the two warp threads and the extra weft thread together. Tie these in a knot as close to the first bead as possible. Repeat this on the other end.

Friendship Pins

Another fun project is making a friendship pin. It is easy to make. You just need a safety pin and small seed beads.
1. Open the safety pin.
2. Thread on as many beads as will fit. You choose the colors and the patterns.
3. To display them on your shoelaces, slip one side of the safety pin under the bottom shoelace of your sneaker. Close the safety pin.

Then you can trade them with your friends.

2. You can close your bracelet by tying the ends in a knot, making it just wide enough to slip over your hand. If you want to be able to take it on and off more easily, you can create a sliding clasp with another bead.

3. To do this, thread all the strings on both ends through another bead. Pull it tight to the end of the beaded part of the bracelet. Tie a small knot on each string about an inch from the bead, and cut off the extra thread. Pull the bead down to widen the bracelet. Slip the bracelet on your wrist. Push the bead up to tighten the bracelet.

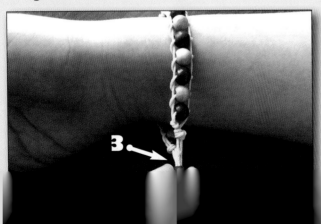

Keeping the Beads Organized
A bead box with compartments can help you keep your beads separated and organized. If you do not have one, you can use an egg carton instead.

This is an example of a box used to organize small objects like beads.

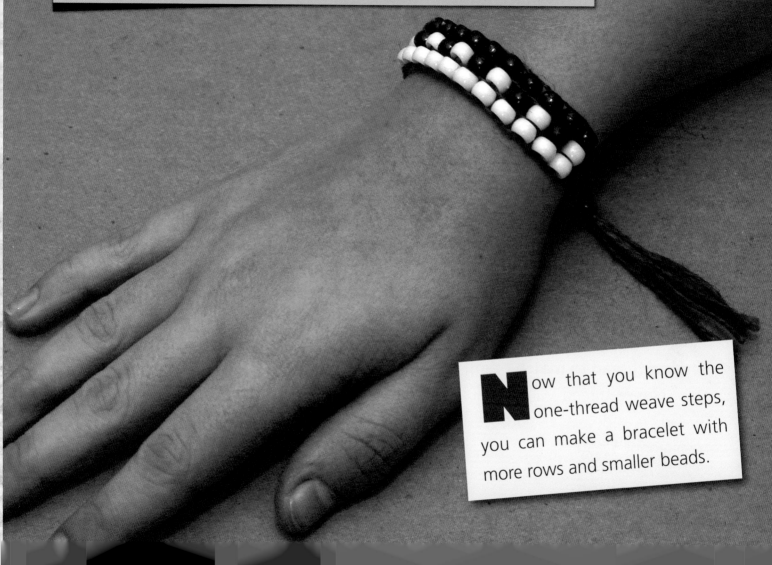

Expanding the Basic Bracelet

Now that you know the one-thread weave steps, you can make a bracelet with more rows and smaller beads.

These are the materials you will need to make a multi-row bracelet:

✓ **Seed beads** Seed beads are also called rocailles [roh-KIE] . These come in tubes or in bags. A tube of seed beads costs about $2.00. A bag is about $1.50.

✓ **One pony bead**

✓ **Beading needle**

✓ **Hemp cord** For this bracelet, you will use hemp for the warp threads.

✓ **Sewing thread to match hemp color** This thinner thread will be your weft thread. A spool of all-purpose thread costs about $2.50.

✓ **Measuring tape**

✓ **Masking tape**

✓ **Bow loom**

✓ **Scissors**

You Are Sitting on My Loom!
You can use the underside of a stool as a loom, too. Flip the stool over and tape the warp threads to one side. Pull them tight and tape them to the other side. Now you can reach your work from above, below, and from the sides.

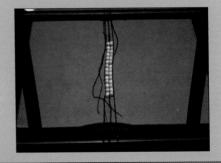

Make a Multi-Row Bracelet

Step #1: Setting Up the Loom

1. This bracelet will have four warp threads. Cut the warp threads to the length described in the basic bracelet instructions. (See Step #1, 1–3, on p. 24)

2. Create a loom like the one described in the basic bracelet instructions. But this time, cut four slots ¼ inch (6.5mm) apart. (See Step #3, 1 on p. 27) Slide all four warp threads onto the loom and hold them in place with tape.

3. Thread the sewing thread onto your beading needle. Cut this thread so it is about three times the length of your warp threads. It will need to be a little longer than the previous project because it will have to weave through more beads. You can always add more weft thread as you go along, however.

4. Tie the end of the weft thread to Warp Thread One, and push to the top. Tuck the tail through one of the warp thread slots.

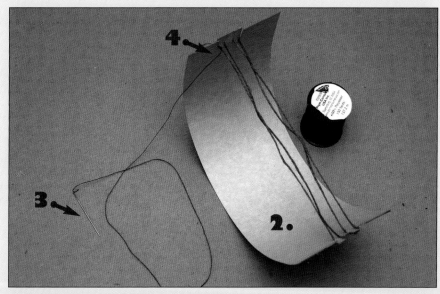

Step #2: Weaving the Beads

1. Just like before, pass the needle end of the weft thread under all the warp threads and toward the right. But this time, string three beads on the weft thread. Hold them in place between the four warp threads with your finger.

2. Now pass the needle back toward the left. It needs to pass over all the warp threads and go back through each bead.

3. Now the needle of the weft thread has returned to the left side. Pull tight so all your beads are securely in place between the warp threads.

4. Continue passing the needle under the warp threads to the right, stringing on the three beads, then pass the needle back through the beads and over the warp threads to the left.

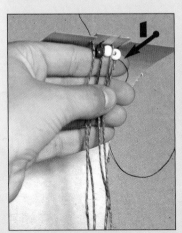
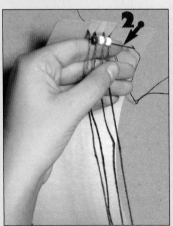
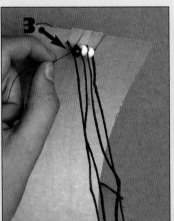
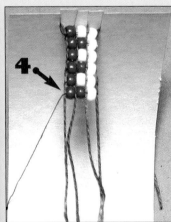

Step #3: Finishing Up

1. When you finish weaving on the beads, tie off the weft thread in a knot on the first warp thread and trim the end. Slip the warp threads off the loom, and tie knots at each end close to the beaded part.

2. To make the clasp, thread all eight strings through a pony bead. As with the one-row bracelet, you can tie small knots at the end of each string to keep the bead from coming off. Move the bead up and down to loosen and tighten the bracelet.

Experiment with different types of string and beads using this weaving technique. Use your imagination to create unlimited types of bracelets.

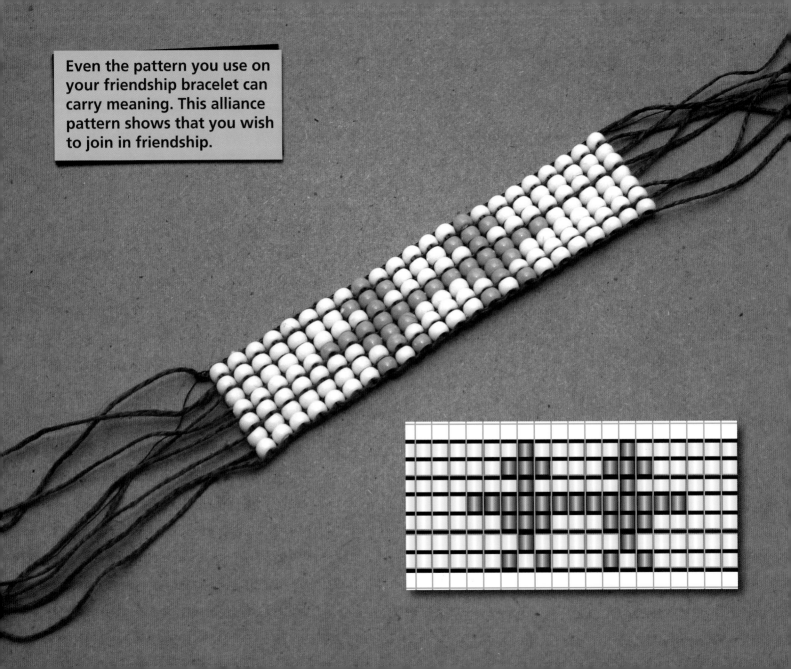

Even the pattern you use on your friendship bracelet can carry meaning. This alliance pattern shows that you wish to join in friendship.

Chapter 4

More Detail:
Playing with Patterns and Beads

Now that you have mastered the basic bracelet, you can play with patterns. With a piece of graph paper, you can plan your bracelet's design by using one square to signify one bead.

First, decide how many warp threads your bracelet will have. Mark the warp thread lines on the graph paper.

With colored pencils, plan your design. For a checkerboard, choose two colors of beads, and alternate them. A chevron pattern is a V shape. You can

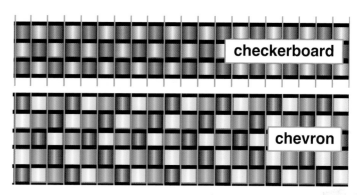

checkerboard

chevron

do this if you have an odd number of rows, at least three.

To show an "alliance" or friendship, as the Native Americans wove into their belts, you can make a people pattern. A simple body and head with arms and legs can be a symbol for a person. If you make two of them holding hands, that means friendship.

Beads Everywhere!

You can buy all sorts of beads. But you can make your own beads, too. In fact, you can turn some unexpected items from indoors and outdoors into beads.

Perhaps you and your friend like to climb a big oak tree in the park. Why not use acorns as beads? If you both like the beach, you can make beads from shells, pebbles, or sea glass. Sea glass is a piece of broken glass that has

Yummy Bracelets

Almost anything can be a bead. Hard candy rings can be beads. So can round oat cereal. You can munch on your bracelet when you get hungry for a snack.

Candy like this can make an edible bracelet.

Shells on woven cords add fun dangles to this bracelet.

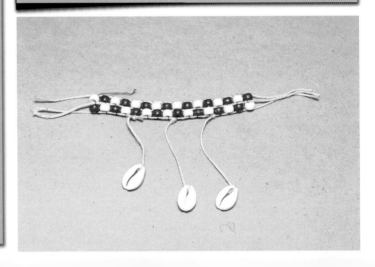

been tumbled smooth by the ocean's waves.

Nuts, seeds, corn kernels, and beans can all make good beads, too.

Check inside your home. Buttons from an old shirt can be made into beads. Even tube-shaped pasta, such as macaroni, from the kitchen can be strung onto a bracelet.

Some of these beads, such as tube-shaped pasta, already have holes in them. For others, you may have to drill a hole to make a bead. With an adult's help, you can drill holes into wood and even shells. But you cannot drill easily into a pebble or a piece of sea glass. Instead, you can make a wire cage for it. In the craft store, you can find craft

Pebbles can be added to bracelets by using metal wire.

wire in all sorts of colors. Wrap it around the pebble to create a loop for threading. These unusual beads can either be part of the bracelet or act as charms hanging off the edges.

How to Make Paper Bugle Beads

You can even make tube-shaped bugle beads out of paper.

These are the materials you will need to make paper bugle beads:

✓ Colorful pictures from magazines, or any kind of scrap paper

✓ Pencil

✓ Ruler

✓ Scissors

✓ Wooden skewers or toothpicks

✓ White glue

1. First, flip through magazines. Look for pages with colorful images, and rip them out. If you want a black and white bracelet, look for pages with lots of text and no pictures.

2. Next, you will need lots of rectangles. With your ruler, measure rectangles on the paper that are about ½ inch (1.3cm) wide by about 5 inches (12.7cm) long. Cut these strips out with scissors.

3. Now lay the paper strip with the side you want to show facing down. Place a skewer on one of the short ends of the rectangle. Roll the strip tightly onto the skewer until you are almost to the end. Adjust the strip as you roll it to be sure it is rolling on straight.

2.

3.

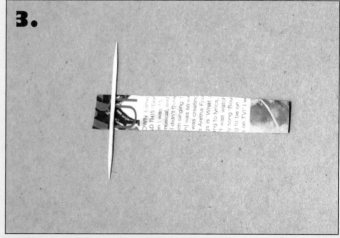

4. Squeeze a dot of glue onto the end of the strip of paper. Continue rolling the strip until the glue holds down the end of the paper. Smear extra glue all over the bead with your finger. The glue will dry clear. This will help seal the bead and keep it from unrolling.

5. Poke the skewer into something to hold it steady, such as a disposable cup, so the bead can dry. It is best to let it dry for a few hours. Remove the bead from the skewer.

5.

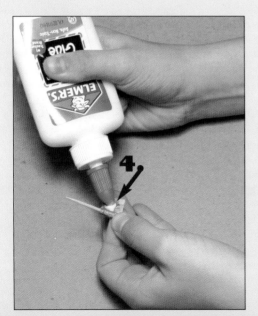

4.

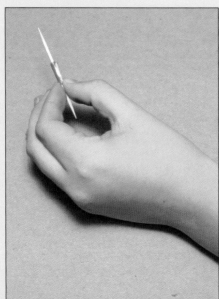

6. Use these beads and the basic bracelet steps described in the previous chapter to make a wampum-style bracelet.

Friendship Day
In 1935 the U.S. Congress set aside a special day for friends. They declared Friendship Day as a national holiday on the first Sunday in August each year. Soon it became a holiday celebrated around the world as well.

On Friendship Day, people exchange cards and gifts. They do something special for each other. A great way to celebrate this holiday is to make a gift for a friend—how about a friendship bracelet?

6.

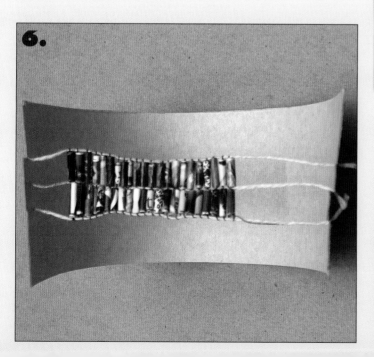

Sharing Your Bracelet

After all of your hard work and the time it took to make a bracelet, now it is time to share it. How will you give it to a friend? You can wrap it up like a gift. You can wear it, and then when your friend admires it, you can give it to him or her. You can even make two of the same bracelet so you and your friend can match. Or perhaps you can wait until your friend needs some cheering up. A bracelet from you will probably make your friend smile.

What does your bracelet say to your friend? It says you value the friendship enough to take the time to make something for him or her. Some jewelry may cost thousands, or even millions of dollars. Your bracelet, even though it may not cost much to make, is worth much more.

alliance (uh-LIE-uhns): A promise or agreement between two groups to work together.

archaeologists (ahr-kee-AHL-uh-jists): Scientists who study the remains of past cultures.

buckskin (BUHK-skin): The skin of a deer.

cord (kohrd): A type of thick thread made from twisted strands of fiber.

council (KOWN-suhl): Gatherings of leaders who make the laws and decisions for Native American groups.

counterfeit (KOWN-ter-fit): Fake.

currency (KUR-uhn-see): Money, or an object used as money.

gemstones (JEM-stohnz): Stones that can be cut and polished in a certain way to be used in jewelry.

hostile (HOS-tl): Unfriendly or acting as an enemy.

macramé (MAK-ruh-may): A craft that uses knotted cord to make a pattern.

quahog (KWAW-hawg): A type of clam that lives along the North American coast of the Atlantic Ocean.

symbolized (SIM-buh-lahyzd): Stood for or represented something.

whelk (welk): An ocean creature with a large, spiral-shaped shell.

For More Information

Books

MacDonald, Fiona. *Jewelry and Make-up Through History*. Milwaukee, WI: Gareth Stevens, 2006.

Mooney, Carla. *Get All Tied Up: Tying Knots*. Chicago: Norwood House Press, 2011.

Newcomb, Rain. *The Girls' World Book of Jewelry: 50 Cool Designs to Make*. New York: Lark, 2004.

Reynolds, Helen. *A Fashionable History of Jewelry and Accessories*. Chicago: Heinemann Library, 2003.

Scheunemann, Pam. *Cool Beaded Jewelry*. Edina, MN: ABDO, 2005.

Torres, Laura. *Friendship Bracelets*. Palo Alto, CA: Klutz, 1996.

Web Sites

About Birthstones: Birthstone List (www.about-birthstones.com/birthstone-list.html). Look up your birthstone on the list to find out its history and meaning at this Web site.

All About Gemstones: History of Gems, Diamonds, and Jewelry (www.allaboutgemstones.com/gem_history.html). Follow the timeline on this Web site to see how jewelry has changed throughout history.

American Museum of Natural History: The Nature of Diamonds Exhibit (www.amnh.org/exhibitions/diamonds/). On this Web site, view pictures and descriptions from this museum's exhibit on diamonds and jewelry throughout history.

Wampum and Wampum Belts (www.ganondagan.org/wampum.html). On this Web site, you can read about the importance of wampum to the Haudenosaunee (Iroquois) nation, as well as details about important belts from its history.

Metropolitan Museum of Art: Egyptian Art (www.metmuseum.org/works_of_art/egyptian_art). Visit this Web site to learn more about the Egyptian art and jewelry collection in this famous New York art museum.

NativeTech: Weave a Virtual Wampum Belt (www.nativetech.org/beadwork/wampumgraph/index.html). Learn all about wampum history and weaving techniques at this Web site devoted to the art of Native Americans.

Paper Bead Crafts (www.paperbeadcrafts.com). Learn the basics of paper bead making, and get some tips and ideas from this crafter's Web site.

Index

About the Author

Dana Meachen Rau is the author of more than 250 books for children from preschool to middle school. She spends her days researching, writing, and trying out her projects in her sunny home office in Burlington, Connecticut.